From Rubbish to Riches

Old Clothes

Daniel Nunn

www.raintreepublishers.co.uk
Visit our website to find out more information about Raintree books.

To order:
☎ Phone 0845 6044371
🖷 Fax +44 (0) 1865 312263
🖳 Email myorders@raintreepublishers.co.uk

Customers from outside the UK please telephone +44 1865 312262

Raintree is an imprint of Capstone Global Library Limited, a company incorporated in England and Wales having its registered office at 7 Pilgrim Street, London, EC4V 6LB – Registered company number: 6695582

Edited by Rebecca Rissman, Daniel Nunn, and Sian Smith
Designed by Joanna Hinton-Malivoire
Picture research by Tracy Cummins
Originated by Capstone Global Library Ltd
Printed and bound in China by South China Printing Company Ltd

ISBN 978 1 406 22677 5 (hardback)
15 14 13 12 11
10 9 8 7 6 5 4 3 2 1

ISBN 978 1 406 22684 3 (paperback)
16 15 14 13 12
10 9 8 7 6 5 4 3 2 1

British Library Cataloguing in Publication Data
Nunn, Daniel. Old clothes. – (From rubbish to riches)
   1. Textile crafts 2. Recycling (Waste, etc.)
   746-dc22
A full catalogue record for this book is available from the British Library.

Acknowledgements
We would like to thank the following for permission to reproduce photographs: Heinemann Raintree pp. 6, 9, 10, 11, 12, 13, 14, 15, 16, 17, 18, 19, 20, 21, 23a, 23b (Karon Dubke); istockphoto pp. 4b (© Silke Dietze), 7 (© Serhiy Zavalnyuk), 8a (© Craig Veltri), 8b (© WendellandCarolyn), 22a (© Pamela Moore), 22b (© drflet), 22c (© Kseniya Ragozina), 23c (© Craig Veltri); Shutterstock pp. 4a (© stormur), 5 (© Karina Bakalyan), 23c (© homydesign), 23d (© stormur).

Cover photograph of a sock monkey, a sock puppet, and socks and back cover photographs of a bag and a sock puppet reproduced with permission of Heinemann Raintree (Karon Dubke).

Every effort has been made to contact copyright holders of material reproduced in this book. Any omissions will be rectified in subsequent printings if notice is given to the publisher.

Contents

Some words are shown in bold, **like this**. You can
find them in the glossary on page 23.

What are old clothes?

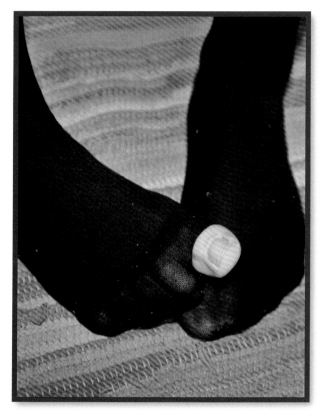

Old clothes are clothes that you don't need any more.

They might have holes in them, or you might just have grown out of them.

Old clothes can be made of different **materials**.

These jumpers are made of wool.

What happens when you throw old clothes away?

Everybody needs clothes.

But when you have finished with them, do you throw them away?

When you throw clothes away they end up at a rubbish tip.

They will be buried in the ground and may stay there for a very long time.

What is recycling?

Old clothes can be **recycled** if you put them in a clothing bank.

When something is recycled it is broken down and used to make something new.

Clothes that you no longer want can also be given to **charity**.

Charities can sell your old clothes or give them to people who need them.

How can I reuse old clothes?

You can also use old clothes to make your own new things.

When you have finished with an item of clothing, put it somewhere safe.

Soon you will have lots of old clothes waiting to be reused.

You are ready to turn your rubbish into riches!

What can I make with old tights?

You can use old tights to make a snake.

You can fill the inside of your snake with old clothes too!

This flying disk has also been made of old tights.

You can throw it like a frisbee.

What can I make with old T-shirts?

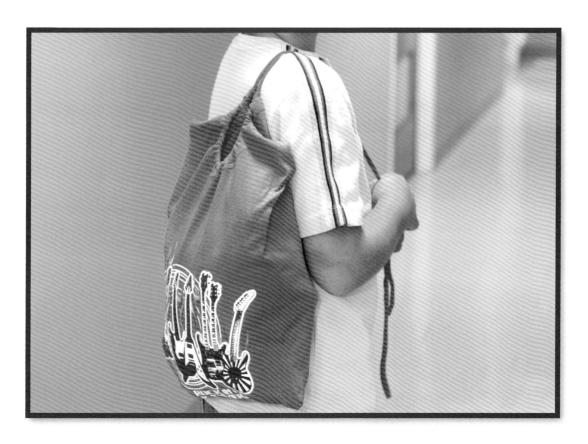

Old T-shirts can be really useful.

This T-shirt has been made into a bag.

Old T-shirts can even be made into jewellery!

This girl's necklace and bracelets have been made from an old T-shirt.

What can I make with old trousers?

This bag is made out of an old pair of jeans!

It is a great way to reuse old trousers with a hole in the knee.

You can also turn an old trouser leg into a **draught excluder**.

This can help keep your bedroom warm on a windy winter day.

Make your own sock puppet

It is easy to make a fun puppet out of an old sock.

You will need a large sock, some **felt**, googly eyes, wool, scissors, and glue.

your fingers
go in here

your thumb
goes in here

First, pull the sock over your hand.

Your fingers will be the puppet's head and your thumb will be the puppet's mouth.

Cut a tongue out of red **felt**.

If you do not have any googly eyes, you can make these out of black and white felt.

Glue the eyes, wool, and the tongue
on to your puppet's head.

Your puppet is finished!

Recycling quiz

One of these items is made from **recycled** clothes. Can you guess which one? (Answer on page 24.)

Glossary

 **charity** organization that raises money to help people or animals in need

 **draught excluder** long, thin cushion placed along the bottom of a door to stop wind blowing into a room

 **felt** type of cloth, often used in crafts

 **material** what something is made of

 **recycle** break down a material and use it again to make something new

Find out more

Ask an adult to help you make fun things with old clothes using the websites below.

Flying disk: **www.makingfriends.com/recycle/ recycled_tights_frisbee.htm**

Bag: **www.craftsforkids.com/projects/ 1100/1108/1108_4.htm**

Snake: **www.freekidscrafts.com/sleepy_snake_from_ pantyhose-e95.html**

Find other ideas at: **www.freekidscrafts.com/recycled_ clothes_crafts_for_kids_|_recycled_crafts-t72.html**

Answer to question on page 22
The bag is made from recycled clothes.

Index